NATURE'S MONSTERS

DINOSAURS

ARMORED & SPIKED DINOSAURS

Per Christiansen

Gareth Stevens
Publishing

Please visit our web site at www.garethstevens.com
For a free color catalog describing Gareth Stevens Publishing's
list of high-quality books, call 1-800-542-2595 (USA)
or 1-800-387-3178 (Canada).
Gareth Stevens Publishing's fax: 1-877-542-2596

Library of Congress Cataloging-in-Publication Data
available upon request from publisher.

ISBN-10: 0-8368-9216-X (lib. bdg.)
ISBN-13: 978-0-8368-9216-1 (lib. bdg.)

This North American edition first published in 2009 by
Gareth Stevens Publishing
A Weekly Reader® Company
1 Reader's Digest Road
Pleasantville, NY 10570-7000 USA

Illustrations:
4–9 © Amber Books Ltd; 10–29 © International Masters Publishers AB

Project Editor: James Bennett
Design: Tony Cohen

Gareth Stevens Senior Managing Editor: Lisa M. Herrington
Gareth Stevens Editor: Joann Jovinelly
Gareth Stevens Creative Director: Lisa Donovan
Gareth Stevens Designer: Paul Bodley

Printed in the United States of America

1 2 3 4 5 6 7 8 9 10 09 08

Contents

Continents of the World

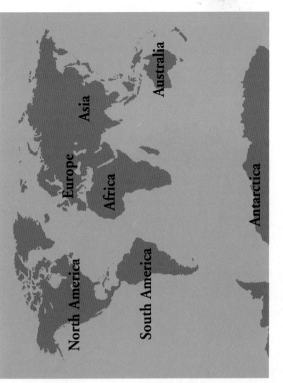

The world is divided into seven continents — North America, South America, Europe, Africa, Asia, Australia, and Antarctica. In this book, the area where each animal lives is shown in red, while all land is shown in green.

Words that appear in the glossary are printed in **boldface** type the first time they occur in the text.

Scelidosaurus

Scelidosaurus (SKEL-eye-doh-SAWR-us) had tough, leathery skin with hard, bony plates. Bony plates helped protect the dinosaur from **predators**.

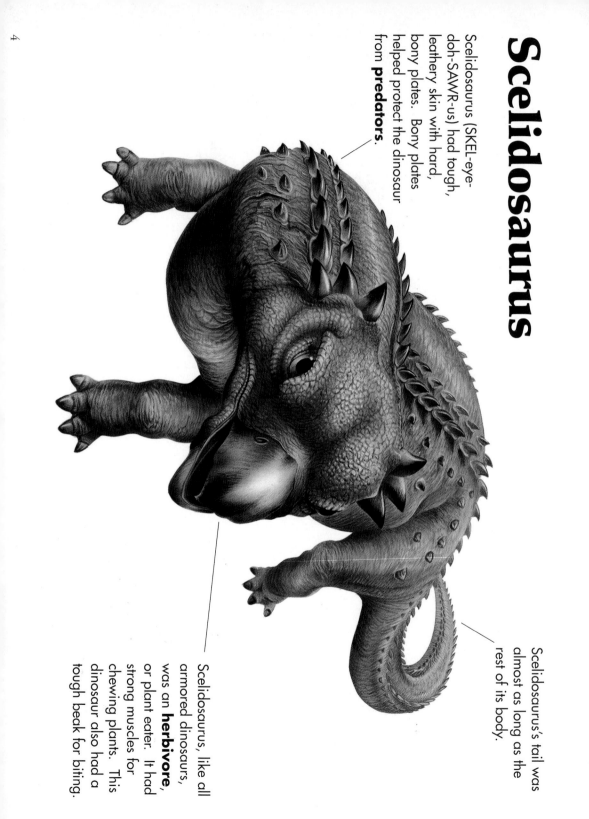

Scelidosaurus's tail was almost as long as the rest of its body.

Scelidosaurus, like all armored dinosaurs, was an **herbivore**, or plant eater. It had strong muscles for chewing plants. This dinosaur also had a tough beak for biting.

Early armored dinosaurs such as **Scelidosaurus** were about 13 feet (4 meters) long. Over time, they grew larger and developed more bony plates on their bodies. The plates helped them defend themselves against predators.

Size

Where in the World

Scelidosaurus lived in Europe during the early **Jurassic** period, about 200 million years ago. Its relatives lived in North America and Asia.

1 Scelidosaurus had less armor than armored dinosaurs that were born later, such as **stegosaurs** and **ankylosaurs.**

2 Stegosaurs had large bony plates along their backs and spikes on the tips of their tails.

3 Ankylosaurs were the most protected of all the armored dinosaurs. They had large plates covering their backs and huge bony clubs at the tips of their tails.

Kentrosaurus

Kentrosaurus (Ken-tro-SORE-us) had two rows of large spikes along its back. These spikes provided good protection against attacking **theropods**.

Kentrosaurus had a small head. Although this dinosaur was an herbivore, its small teeth probably made chewing plants difficult. Kentrosaurus lived alongside other plant eaters such as Barosaurus and Brachiosaurus.

Like most stegosaurs, Kentrosaurus had hind legs that were longer and more powerful than its front legs.

Kentrosaurus also had spikes on its tail.

Kentrosaurus was a medium-sized stegosaur. It was about 15 feet (4.6 meters) long. Kentrosaurus did not weigh more than 1,000 pounds (454 kilograms). Although it was small in size, its armor could be deadly.

Size

Did You Know?

Most of what we know about Kentrosaurus comes from a African fossil site in the United Republic of Tanzania. At the site, scientists found several Kentrosaurus skeletons. Because the skeletons were upright, these dinosaurs likely got trapped in deep mud and died standing up!

Where in the World

Kentrosaurus lived in East Africa during the late Jurassic period, about 150 million years ago.

Smaller dinosaurs like Kentrosaurus were not always easy targets. This meat-eating Allosaurus may think that it has stumbled upon an easy **prey**, but Kentrosaurus defends itself with its huge spikes.

Ankylosaurus

Ankylosaurus (An-kill-oh-SORE-us) was covered in tough, bony plates. This massive armor protected the dinosaur against predators.

Ankylosaurus's underside and legs did not have armor. These areas were at risk of attack.

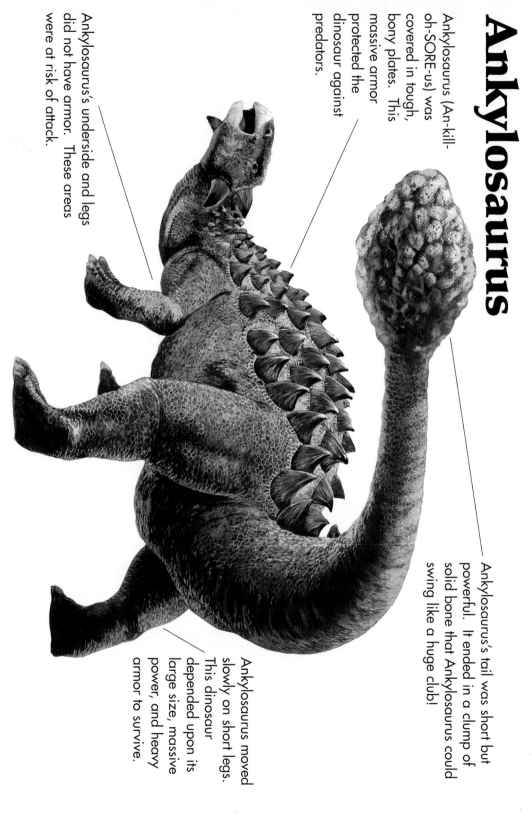

Ankylosaurus's tail was short but powerful. It ended in a clump of solid bone that Ankylosaurus could swing like a huge club!

Ankylosaurus moved slowly on short legs. This dinosaur depended upon its large size, massive power, and heavy armor to survive.

Ankylosaurus was one of the the largest ankylosaurs. It was 30 feet (9 m) long and weighed 6 short tons (5.4 metric tons). Newly hatched ankylosaurs were much smaller.

1 Ankylosaurus lived alongside terrifying predators like the mighty tyrannosaurus. Although Ankylosaurus was a peaceful plant eater, it was extremely dangerous, even to a fully grown tyrannosaur.

Ankylosaurus was wide across the hips — as much as 6 feet (1.8 m). With such a wide, heavy body and short legs, Ankylosaurus could not be tipped over by a predator. Modern army vehicles use the same design. They are also wide and heavy so they cannot tip over easily.

Ankylosaurus lived in North America in the late **Cretaceous** period, about 67 million years ago. Close relatives lived in Europe and Asia.

2 When attacked, Ankylosaurus bent its knees so its soft underbelly was close to the ground. This way, the dinosaur could not be bitten. Even a tyrannosaur could not crack the armor along Ankylosaurus's back. When Ankylosaurus swung its tail directly at a tyrannosaur, the force of the swing was often deadly!

Gastonia

Gastonia (Gas-TOE-knee-uh) had bony spikes on its back and along the sides of its body. The spikes were useful to protect against attack.

Like other ankylosaurs, Gastonia had no protection on its legs or underbelly.

Gastonia had large and small plates on its skin.

Gastonia's legs were powerful, but its feet were short and heavy, like those of a modern rhinoceros.

Gastonia was a large, heavy ankylosaur. It grew to about 20 feet (6 m) long and weighed nearly 3 short tons (2.7 m tons).

Size

Gastonia lived in North America during the mid-Cretaceous period, about 100 million years ago. Close relatives lived in Europe and Mongolia.

Did You Know?

Ankylosaurids and nodosaurids were both types of ankylosaurs. Ankylosaurids had huge bony clubs at the end of their tails and small spikes along their backs and sides. Nodosaurids like Gastonia had only spikes on their sides.

1 Like all ankylosaurs, Gastonia was a plant eater. It fed on low-growing ferns and shrubs, which it bit off with its tough, horny beak. This pair of hunting tyrannosaurs spots Gastonia eating.

2 Hoping for a tasty meal, one of the tyrannosaurs tries to attack Gastonia. But Gastonia was not easy prey. Its back was well protected, and it could use the spikes on its sides to stab a tyrannosaur's legs!

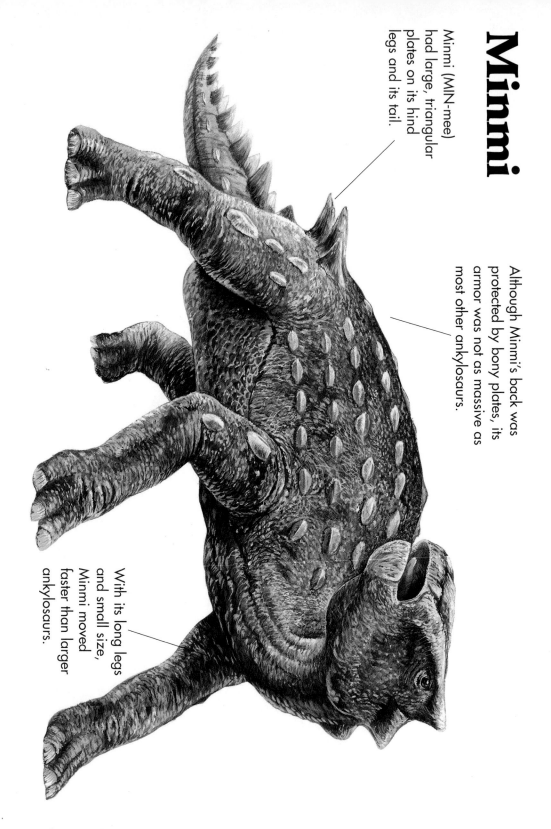

Minmi

Minmi (MIN-mee) had large, triangular plates on its hind legs and its tail.

Although Minmi's back was protected by bony plates, its armor was not as massive as most other ankylosaurs.

With its long legs and small size, Minmi moved faster than larger ankylosaurs.

Minmi was a small ankylosaur. It was less than 10 feet (3 m) long and weighed no more than 400 pounds (181 kg). Minmi's small size was an advantage because it could find shelter from predators.

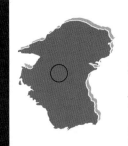

Size

Minmi lived in Australia during the mid-Cretaceous period, about 100 million years ago.

1 Minmi lived alone. It probably stayed close to lakes, rivers, and the ocean, where it could find low-growing plants such as ferns and horsetails. It used its horny, narrow beak to break off plant leaves and stems. Minmi had a wide skull, but scientists believe it had the smallest brain of all the dinosaurs.

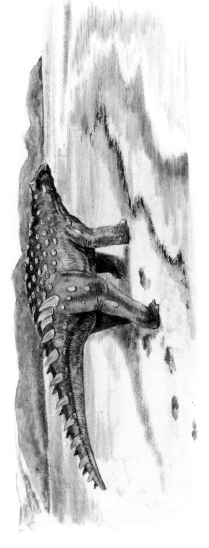

2 Scientists know very little about the **environment** in which Minmi lived. Predators were probably rare, and several of them were too small to be much of a threat. Few enemies could be the reason why Minmi had so little armor. Unlike other ankylosaurs, it did not need it.

Nodosaurus

Nodosaurus (No-doe-SORE-us) had armor on its back and neck. Predators could not bite through these bony plates.

Nodosaurus had less armor on its head than other large ankylosaurs.

Spikes on Nodosaurus's body and tail could be used as powerful weapons.

Nodosaurus's legs were strong, but short. This dinosaur could not move quickly.

Nodosaurus was a large nodosaurid. It was 20 feet (6 m) long and weighed 2 short tons (1.8 m tons). This ankylosaur's huge size and thick armor were important defenses against hungry tyrannosaurs.

Size

When tyrannosaurs attacked Nodosaurus, it dropped to the ground to protect its soft belly. Tyrannosaurs could not flip over its wide, heavy body. Nodosaurus also swung its tail, which had sharp spikes that cut deep gashes in the legs of predators.

Nodosaurus lived in North America in the late Cretaceous period, about 75 million years ago. Several close relatives lived in North America and other parts of the world, such as northern Asia.

Sauropelta

Sauropelta (SAWR-oh-PELL-tuh) did not have a bony club on its tail.

Although Sauropelta had long legs, it moved slowly because of its armor.

Sauropelta's large shoulder spikes helped defend it against hungry theropods.

Sauropelta had a smaller head than other large nodosaurids.

Sauropelta was a close relative of Nodosaurus, and they were about the same size. Sauropelta was 20 feet (6 m) long, but was more slender, weighing 1.5 short tons (1.4 m tons).

Sauropelta was one of the few nodosaurids with huge spikes on its shoulders. Scientists know that the spikes defended Sauropelta against its attackers, but they are not certain how the dinosaur used them. Scientists believe that Sauropelta may have forced its huge spikes into the belly of an attacking predator. A direct hit would have been deadly.

Size

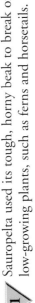

1 Sauropelta used its tough, horny beak to break off low-growing plants, such as ferns and horsetails.

2 Like other ankylosaurs, Sauropelta had small teeth. It could not chew its food well, so it swallowed it whole. Plants are tough to **digest**, but Sauropelta and other ankylosaurs had very large **intestines**, where plants **fermented**. Fermentation is a common way of breaking down food, but it produces a lot of gas!

Where in the World

Sauropelta lived in North America in the mid-Cretaceous period, about 120 to 95 million years ago.

Saichania

Saichania (Sigh-CHAIN-ee-uh) was a giant ankylosaur. It had a short, powerful tail that ended in a huge, bony club.

Saichania's tail was formed from separate pieces of bone. They **fused** together to form a solid club, an excellent weapon against attackers.

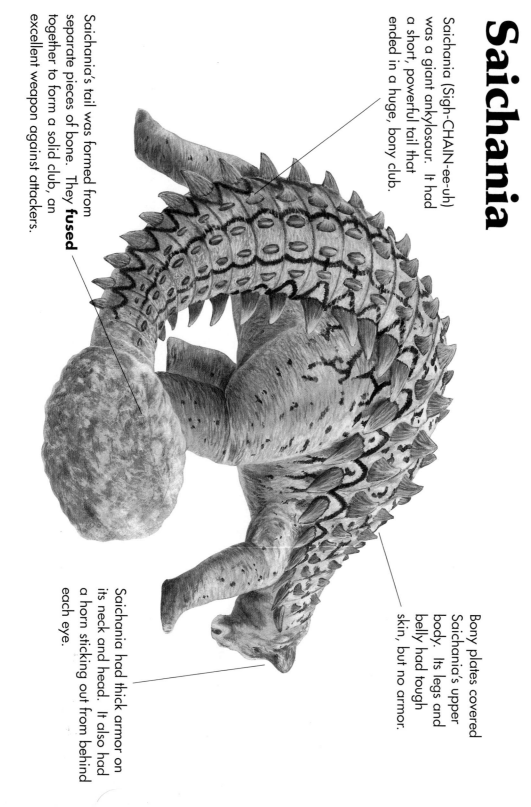

Bony plates covered Saichania's upper body. Its legs and belly had tough skin, but no armor.

Saichania had thick armor on its neck and head. It also had a horn sticking out from behind each eye.

Saichania was 25 feet (7.6 m) long and weighed more than 4 short tons (3.6 m tons). Few ankylosaurs grew so large.

Size

1 Saichania lived in desert environments that had sandstorms. Scientists have found fossilized remains of dinosaurs that died during these storms. Because these dinosaurs often became buried in sand within minutes, their fossils are well preserved.

2 Scientists have also found fossilized remains of Saichania babies. A sandstorm quickly buried these dinosaurs in their nest.

Saichania lived in the dry, deserts of northern Asia in the late Cretaceous period — about 75 million years ago. It had close relatives, such as Ankylosaurus, in other parts of the world.

Struthiosaurus

Struthiosaurus (STROOTH-ee-oh-SAWR-us) had large spikes along the sides of its body.

Struthiosaurus had long legs for an ankilosaur. Because Struthiosaurus weighed less than most ankilosaurs, it did not need such sturdy legs.

A thick, bony plate protected the top of Struthiosaurus's head.

Struthiosaurus was a plant eater. It had a narrow mouth with upper and lower teeth that met in an exact way when chewing. This design was useful for grinding leaves.

Struthiosaurus was one of the smallest ankylosaurs. It grew no longer than 10 feet (3 m), and it weighed about 350 pounds (160 kg).

Size

1 Struthiosaurus lived in central Europe. Millions of years ago, this part of the world was much different. Instead of being one continent, it was broken up into several islands.

Struthiosaurus lived in central Europe during the late Cretaceous period, about 70 million years ago. Its fossil remains have also been found in Romania, but it probably lived in other areas as well.

2 Because islands have limited amounts of food, they often cannot support large animals. Scientists believe the small Struthiosaurus was well suited to island survival.

Dacentrurus

Dacentrurus (DAY-sen-TROO-rus) had large, pointed plates on its back for protection from predators. The plates on its neck were shorter.

Like all stegosaurs, Dacentrurus had front legs that were shorter and less powerful than its hind legs.

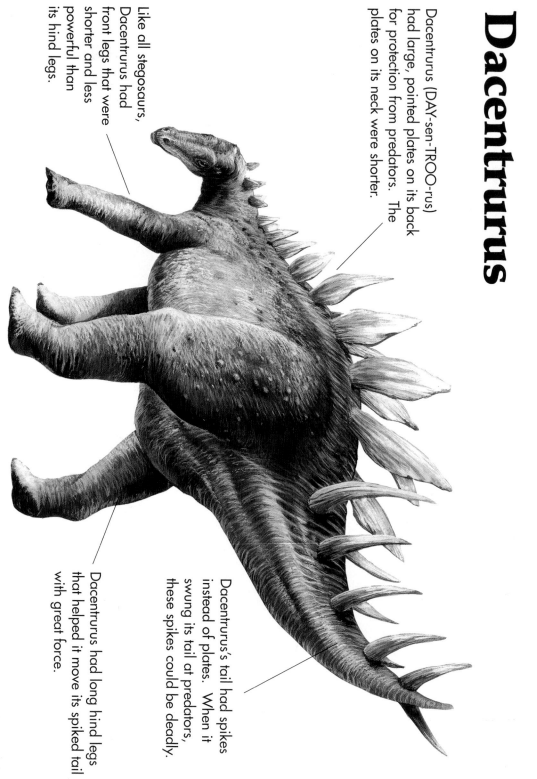

Dacentrurus's tail had spikes instead of plates. When it swung its tail at predators, these spikes could be deadly.

Dacentrurus had long hind legs that helped it move its spiked tail with great force.

Dacentrurus was a large stegosaur. It grew to 20 feet (6 m) and could weigh more than 2 short tons (1.8 m tons) — about the same size as a large sport utility vehicle (SUV).

Size

1 ▶ Dacentrurus used its mighty spiked tail to guard against terrifying predators, such as the monstrous Allosaurus.

2 ▶ Dacentrurus whipped its spiked tail toward this young Allosaurus. After dodging the blow, the predator moved on, leaving Dacentrurus alone to feed.

Where in the World

Fossil remains of Dacentrurus have also been found in England, France, and Spain. Dacentrurus lived during the late Jurassic period, about 160 to 150 million years ago.

Huayangosaurus

Huayangosaurus (Hwa-yang-o-SORE-us) had a larger and wider head than most other stegosaurs. It had teeth for chewing plants, but later stegosaurs did not.

Stegosaurs that lived in later periods had shorter front legs than Huayangosaurus.

Huayangosaurus probably used its shoulder spikes against predators.

Huayangosaurus had two pairs of spikes at the tip of its tail. It used these spikes to defend itself.

Huayangosaurus was a primitive stegosaur and one of the smallest. It was 15 feet (4.6 m) long, and it weighed 1,500 pounds (680 kg).

Size

Huayangosaurus lived in what is now China during the mid-Jurassic period, about 175 million years ago. Since it is one of the earliest known stegosaurs, scientists believe stegosaurs may be **native** to Asia.

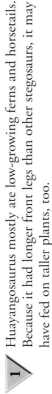

1 Huayangosaurus mostly ate low-growing ferns and horsetails. Because it had longer front legs than other stegosaurs, it may have fed on taller plants, too.

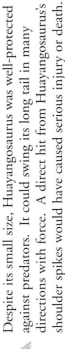

2 Despite its small size, Huayangosaurus was well-protected against predators. It could swing its long tail in many directions with force. A direct hit from Huayangosaurus's shoulder spikes would have caused serious injury or death.

Tuojiangosaurus

Tuojiangosaurus (Too-oh-gee-ANG-oh-SAWR-us) had large spikes and plates sticking out from its back. These spikes and plates were not a part of its skeleton. They were separate bones that grew from the skin and that were covered by flesh.

Like Stegosaurus, Tuojiangosaurus had many small bones in its skin along the neck and shoulder.

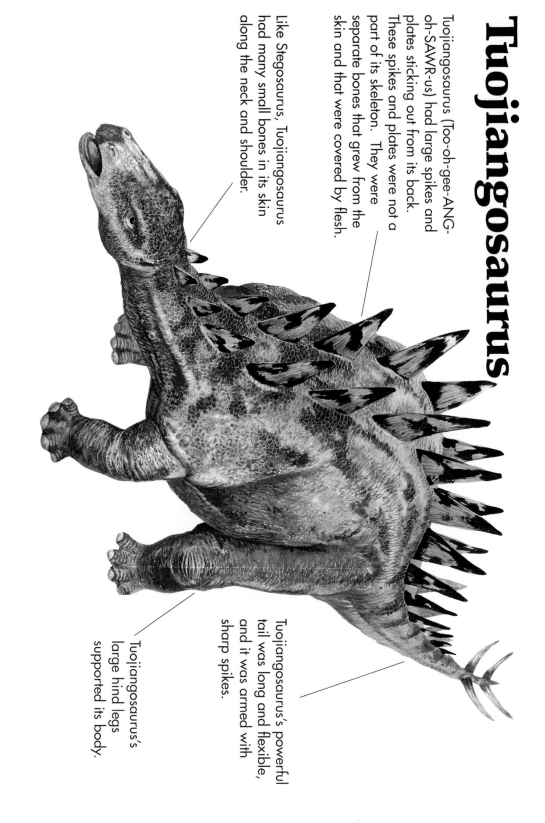

Tuojiangosaurus's powerful tail was long and flexible, and it was armed with sharp spikes.

Tuojiangosaurus's large hind legs supported its body.

The name Tuojiangosaurus means "Tuo River lizard." This plant-eating dinosaur was 23 feet (7 m) long.

Size

Stegosaurs are known for having big spikes — and tiny brains. The huge Tuojiangosaurus had a brain no larger than a fist! Scientists once thought it had a second brain inside its pelvis, but it was probably a mass of nerves, not a real brain. These nerves may have controlled the dinosaur's legs and tail.

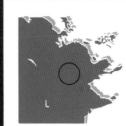

Tuojiangosaurus was part of a rich variety of dinosaurs that lived in Asia. Tuojiangosaurus lived during the late Jurassic period, about 155 to 145 million years ago.

1 Tuojiangosaurus did not usually attack other dinosaurs, but it lived alongside some large theropods. Tuojiangosaurus needed its plates and spikes to stay alive.

2 A Sinraptor rushes toward a startled Tuojiangosaurus, but it has made a serious mistake. Instead of sneaking up from behind, it has attacked the dinosaur from the side. Tuojiangosaurus swings its tail and delivers a bone-shattering blow to the theropod's ribs.

Lexovisaurus

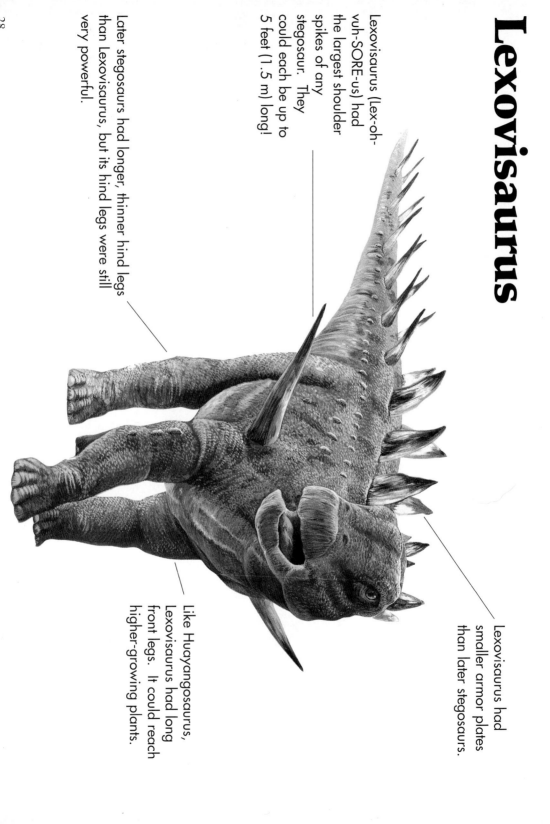

Lexovisaurus (lex-oh-vuh-SORE-us) had the largest shoulder spikes of any stegosaur. They could each be up to 5 feet (1.5 m) long!

Later stegosaurs had longer, thinner hind legs than Lexovisaurus, but its hind legs were still very powerful.

Lexovisaurus had smaller armor plates than later stegosaurs.

Like Huayangosaurus, Lexovisaurus had long front legs. It could reach higher-growing plants.

Lexovisaurus was a medium-sized stegosaur. It was 15 feet (4.6 m) long and weighed about 2,000 pounds (907 kg). Lexovisaurus was a relative of Huayangosaurus, a smaller stegosaur.

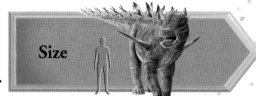

Size

Did You Know?

Later stegosaurs were better able to defend themselves. Their legs were shorter and their bodies were closer to the ground. Because it was easier for them to turn around on their hind legs, they could keep their spiky tails pointed at predators.

1 Lexovisaurus and Huayangosaurus were both primitive stegosaurs. They had wider mouths and larger heads than later stegosaurs, so they ate a greater variety of plants.

2 Later stegosaurs had smaller heads and narrower mouths. They probably had a limited diet.

3 The last stegosaurs had even smaller heads and pointed mouths. They were likely very selective about the plants they ate.

Lexovisaurus lived during the middle and late Jurassic period, between 170 and 155 million years ago. Its fossil remains have been found in England and France.

Glossary

ancestor — people or animals in a family or group who lived in earlier times

ankylosaurs — large, plant-eating dinosaurs that usually had bony plates or spikes sticking up on their backs and spikes on the tips of their tails

Cretaceous — a period of time from about 144 to 65 million years ago when dinosaurs roamed Earth

digest — to break down food in the stomach and intestines so it can be used by the body for energy

environment — the place where a plant or animal lives

fermented — the process of being broken down into different chemicals

fossil — remains or imprints of animals and dinosaurs from an earlier time, often prehistoric; fossils are found beneath Earth's surface, pressed into rocks

fused — combined together

herbivore — a plant-eater

intestines — tube-like parts of the body through which food passes after it is eaten and leaves the stomach

Jurassic — a period of time from 206 to 144 million years ago, when dinosaurs roamed the Earth and when birds first appeared

Latin — the language of the ancient Romans, which scientists use to name plants and animals

native — the place or environment where a person or creature was born or came into being

pelvis — the part of a skeleton that connects the spine to the legs in humans and to the hind legs in animals

predators — animals that hunt and kill other animals for food

prey — an animal hunted and killed for food

primitive — being the first or earliest of its kind in existence

stegosaurs — large, plant-eating dinosaurs that had thick bony plates covering their backs and large bony clubs at the tips of their tails

theropods — meat-eating dinosaurs that walked on two legs and ranged in size from small to very large

vertebrae — the series of bones that join together to make up the backbone

For More Information

Books

Armored Dinosaurs. Meet the Dinosaurs (series).
Don Lessem (Lerner, 2005)

Armored, Plated, and Bone-Headed Dinosaurs: The Ankylosaurs, Stegosaurs, and Pachycephalosaurs. The Dinosaur Library (series). Thom and Laurie Holmes (Enslow, 2002)

Dinosaurs! The Biggest, Baddest, Strangest, Fastest. Howard Zimmerman (Atheneum, 2000)

Horned Dinosaurs. Meet the Dinosaurs (series).
Don Lessem (Lerner, 2004)

Outside and Inside Dinosaurs. Sandra Markle (Aladdin, 2003)

Tricerratops and Other Horned and Armored Dinosaurs. Dinosaurs Alive! (series). Jinny Johnson (Smart Apple Media, 2007)

Web Sites

Dinosaur Expedition
www.projectexploration.org

Dinosauria
www.ucmp.berkeley.edu/diapsids/dinosaur.html

Dinosaur Illustrations
www.search4dinosaurs.com

Dinosaur Time Machine
www.mantyweb.com/dinosaur

KidsDinos.com – Dinosaurs For Kids
www.kidsdinos.com

Paleontology Portal
www.paleoportal.org

Zoom Dinosaurs
www.enchantedlearning.com/subjects/dinosaurs

Publisher's note to educators and parents: Our editors have carefully reviewed these web sites to ensure that they are suitable for children. Many web sites change frequently, however, and we cannot guarantee that a site's future contents will continue to meet our high standards of quality and educational value. Be advised that children should be closely supervised whenever they access the Internet.

Index